10 Best Parenting Ways to Ruin Your Teenager

Israel Galindo

Don Reagan

Published by Educational Consultants
www.galindoconsultants.com

ISBN 0-9715765-5-6

A FREE EIGHT-SESSION GROUP **STUDY GUIDE** FOR THIS BOOK IS AVAILABLE FROM THE EDUCATIONAL CONSULTANTS WEB SITE: www.galindoconsultants.com

Printed in the United States by Morris Publishing
3212 East Highway 30
Kearney, NE 68847
1-800-650-7888

CONTENTS

INTRODUCTION

Exasperated parents often ask me, "Why is it so hard to parent teenagers?" I sometimes answer by saying, "Well, the short answer is that all teenagers are essentially crazy!" Then I share with them an interesting psychological phenomenon. When teenagers are given psychometric assessments designed for adults (psychological tests that assess cognition, reasoning, logic, and critical thinking), the results come back as if a psychotic subject had taken the test—that is, someone who is out of touch with reality and does not have a capacity for rational thinking.

The reason parenting teenagers can often be so difficult is that they do not think like "normal adults"—they're teenagers, and so they *think* like teenagers! This means that teenagers cannot reason like adults, anticipate the natural consequences of their actions (that ability doesn't fully develop until around age twenty-five!), or understand why certain universal rules of the universe that govern everyone else on the planet applies to them personally (they tend to think that

1

they do not!). In other words, the problem with teenagers is that . . . they are teenagers!

But parenting teenagers does not have to be the angst-filled experience that most parents make it to be. Not if parents understand three fundamental truths of the parent-teenage child relationship:

1. Adolescents are "in transition" from childhood to adulthood. Your relationship with your teenager, therefore, needs to shift from "parenting" to one of *coaching and challenging* during the adolescent years. Your teenager is no longer a child and will not always be a teenager. In other words, adolescence, and the craziness that goes with it, is not a permanent condition. But how you relate to your teenager during these important years will make a big difference.

2. Parenting mistakes happen and they are not fatal, either to the teenager or the parent. No parent is perfect, nor should parents try to pretend to their children that they are. A parent who openly struggles and sometimes fails is a gift to a child, not an obstacle. It is never the occasional "mistake" that shapes us; rather, it is the consistent patterns of relationships that determine personality, attitude, outlook, and behavior. Raising healthy teenagers is hard work, and we occasionally stumble, but it's worth the struggle.

3. Parents do matter to their teenagers. It may not seem like it, but teenagers are watching, listening and learning from their parents. This

does not mean we must do everything right. Parenting is too complex to ever make that a reality. The teenage years can be tough, but throwing up our hands in exasperation and giving up is not the answer. Our teenagers need us, even if they don't know it, and there is much we can do to make the teenage years within our family a less anxious and more productive journey.

The following chapters present the "ten best" parenting ways to ruin your teenager (there are undoubtedly many other ways, but these are the poor practices which we find parents of teenagers tend to be most guilty of). These parenting ways "ruin" teenagers and sabotage our effectiveness as parents when they become a patterned way of relating with our teenagers. Remember, rarely is it the one-time traumatic event that shapes our lives—typically, it is the patterned ways of communicating, relating, and being together that forms values, beliefs, and personal myths. Patterns in behavior can facilitate good relationships, or they can serve to perpetually keep us stuck and at odds with one another.

The format of each chapter is as follows: we present the best parental way to ruin your teenager, then, we explain why that behavior, when it becomes a patterned way of relating to each other in the family, is ruinous to our relationship with our teenagers. Finally, we offer the "rule" to follow related to each of the parenting behaviors under discussion.

For ease of reading, Don and Israel will use "one voice" in this book. The personal illustrations will come from both of our families, but we'll avoid awkwardness in style by writing from a personal perspective without attempting to identify who's who or from which family came the illustration. The personal illustrations we provide involve our boys (we have no daughters). However, the anecdotes illustrate universal relationship principles applicable to all teenagers and their parents, regardless of gender.

One

1. Parent your teenager as if he or she is a child

The consequence of practicing this parenting behavior consistently is that you will frustrate your teenager and will inhibit his or her ability to negotiate the path to adulthood by not allowing your teenager the freedom, responsibility, and risk, of learning how to become an adult.

It's amazing how quickly our children grow up! Every once in a while we turn around and look at them, and realize that they've sprouted a couple of inches (time to take down the hems again!). And, suddenly, one day our sweet little child is a teenager, with all of the accompanying raging hormones that come with that age. For most of us, the transition from childhood to adolescence happens so fast that we are caught by surprise and find ourselves unprepared to make the shift in how we need to function in our parental role. Often, if there is a younger sibling at home, the matter is further complicated when we try to be "fair" by treating all of the siblings the same. But treating children and teenagers the same, in an attempt to "be fair", is actually unfair to both. Children and teenagers are at different developmental stages, and therefore some rules that appropriately apply to the one cannot be applied to the other.

The fact of the matter is that you cannot "parent" your teenager. Parenting is a particular function that is over by the time a child is seven. That is, whatever it is that your child needs from you—those things which he or she cannot get from anyone or anywhere else that constitutes "parenting"—is over very quickly.

Consider these facts: by the time a child is seven years of age...

- He will have learned over half of what he will learn his entire life
- She will have acquired her basic sense of self
- He will have acquired his basic orientation toward the world
- She will have acquired the basic prejudices she will carry for the rest of her life
- He will have attained his basic level of self-esteem
- She will have been inculcated with the basic values that will inform most of her life and influence most of her life decisions
- He will have developed his basic faith orientation
- She will have achieved her basic sexual and gender orientation.

Once your child becomes a teenager, trying to "parent" him or her is an inappropriate and futile exercise. In fact, the more you try to "parent" your teenager, the more you will end up frustrating yourself and your teen. You will always be your child's parent, of course, but your *functioning*—the way you need to relate to your teenager—must change to meet your child's developmental stage. Think about it this way: *When our children become teens we need to be fired as their managers and re-hired as consultants or coaches.*

Making the change from parent to consultant is not easy. Our family recently went camping with several other families on an organized wilderness excursion in central Maine. One of the activities was canoeing on a large lake near our campsite. Our camp leader instructed us to assume roles during this canoe trip that were different from the roles we normally assumed in our families. Given my typical family role, I would normally sit in the back of the canoe where steering can be controlled with a variety of oar strokes. My son would normally sit in the front where he would provide the muscle to power the canoe and take direction from me. This time we swapped positions with me sitting in the front and he in the back. My wife (who often assumes the mediator role) sat in the middle between us but was instructed to remain quiet and not intervene. There were eight canoes in our group. As we set out, seven canoes rowed in the direction of our ultimate destination while one canoe (ours) went in the exact opposite direction.

Immediately the tension in the canoe rose dramatically and I began barking out instructions to correct the situation. My son became very angry with me for so quickly re-assuming my old role and eventually pulled his oar out of the water to wait things out. My wife, with enormous effort, managed to bite her lip and stay out of the struggle between my son and me. After a few tense minutes my son requested that I get back to powering the canoe and that he would get us back on course. If he needed help he would ask for it, but in the meantime he needed me to just row. So, I whirled around in a huff and began rowing—hard. In moments he had the canoe turned in the general direction of the other canoes. As we moved across the lake we occasionally drifted left or right of a straight course and I found myself sneaking in some correcting strokes. My son noticed this and from the back of the canoe I heard "Dad! What are you doing?" Shamed by being caught in such a blatant "control-freak" act I finally stopped trying to manage the situation and let my son take complete responsibility for steering the canoe.

At that point all of us got into a groove and for the rest of our trip we forgot about the bad start and ended up enjoying the beautiful scenery along the lake. Despite our wayward beginning we arrived at our destination at the same time as the other canoes. Having spent many years managing our children, it can be extremely difficult to shift our parental functioning to the coaching and consulting role that our teens need from us.

Pay attention to your teen's posture and attitude the next time you are tempted to "parent" him in some way. The reason your teenager is so recalcitrant in those moments of willful parenting on your part is that he or she is trying to tell you, "Don't try to parent me anymore! You had your chance when I was a child, but that's not what I need now!" Teenagers are in a twilight zone between childhood and adulthood. We can't treat them like children, but as we'll see later, we can't quite treat them like adults, either.

For some time I was confused with my youngest son's recalcitrant behavior about following up with things I asked him to do around the house. It wasn't until he blew up during a confrontation about his apparent irresponsibility that I realized what was behind his behavior. It wasn't that he was belligerently refusing to do what I asked; the issue was that he was frustrated by the WAY I asked. In his eyes I was still "telling him to do things" instead of "asking." To him this felt like a lack of respect. He wanted to be grown up, and wanted to *feel* grown up, and to be treated as such. I learned to adjust my behavior by *asking* him to do things around the house, rather than "ordering" him to do them. In his mind, being "told" to do something felt like I was treating him like a child—when I "asked" him to do something, he felt more respected and felt like it was, in part, his decision to do what needed doing.

The rule to follow in relating to our teenagers is to change our parental posture. Rather than trying to continue to "parent" them in the ways that were formerly appropriate when they were younger, we need to take a different approach. As parents, coaching and challenging are the two postures that work best with teens. The reason is that these postures allow for teaching values and principles about relationships and responsibilities, while also giving teenagers the chance to choose to do the right thing.

Two

2. Treat your teenager as if he or she is an adult.

One common mistake parents make is to treat their teenager as a child, but the other is to treat their teenager as if he or she were an adult. The consequence of consistently practicing this parenting behavior is that you will confuse your teenager by removing too quickly the boundaries he or she needs to learn about the world and about him or herself as a person.

Teenagers are on their way to becoming adults, but they are not there yet. Adolescence is a time of turbulent transition from childhood to adulthood. Most of us tend to ascribe more maturity and competence to our teenagers than they actually have achieved. This is natural, of course. We all think our own children are "special" and "unique," smarter, and more competent than other people's children, don't we? But regardless to what extent that might be true of our own offspring, the fact remains that a teenager remains "stuck in adolescence."

Teenagers think differently because of two factors. First, they are victims of developmental egocentricity; that is, they have great difficulty (and some have an incapacity) to see the world from a perspective other than their own. This does not mean that they are "selfish," although egocentrism sometimes makes it appear so. It just means that at their stage of development teenagers lack the maturity to put themselves "in the other person's shoes." In the words of Erik Erikson, the great psychotherapist, adolescents have an inability for perspective-taking like "I can see you seeing me seeing you."

Second, according to recent brain research, it takes the brain longer to mature than previously believed. For example, the portion of the brain that processes risks and consequences is not fully developed in the adolescent brain. This means that despite understanding "rules," teenagers have difficulty understanding (1) that those rules apply to them, personally and individually, and (2) the very real consequences of not following those rules. This is why, despite more teen driver education and longer waiting periods for issuing driver's licenses to teens, the number one cause of death among adolescents in our country remains auto accidents. Despite countless lectures and lessons on avoiding unsafe driving, speeding, drinking while driving, or about "watching out for the other guy"—and despite the fact that teenagers can recite the litany of "rules" related to driving—the reality is that they often cannot process the consequences of their own behavior when they are behind the wheel. The same is true about using drugs, sexual experimentation, and other risky behaviors.

What it comes down to is this: despite the fact that they are no longer children, there are still some things teenagers cannot decide for themselves. They continue to suffer from egocentric perspectives that do not allow them to understand the consequences of their actions, and therefore, they need our help as parents to coach and challenge them.

One day I received a notice from the city about an overdue, un-paid, parking ticket. I was puzzled because I didn't remember being issued a parking ticket, so I read the notice more carefully. After deciphering the summons I realized that my son must have gotten the ticket around the area of his downtown college campus. When I asked my son about the ticket, he responded, "Oh, yeah. I forgot to tell you." He explained that he had tried to pay for the ticket over the Internet, as per instructions on the summons. When that proved unsuccessful, he intended to pay for it later, but procrastinated. This, of course, was not a major crisis, but I took the opportunity to try to coach my son into seeing beyond what his egocentrism allowed. I explained to him that, while I was happy to provide a car for his use while in college, it was still MY car. Despite his thinking about it as *his* car, the fact is that the car is in MY name and therefore, I am legally responsible for it. I further explained the other consequences I knew he could not envision. I pointed out that if he was irresponsible in paying a ticket issued to the car, that it affected MY credit and MY record, because the car is in MY name. The message that the teenager who is stuck in his or her egocentricism needs to hear is that "It's not just about you. What you do always affects and involves others."

The next time my son received a parking ticket at the downtown campus (a mere two weeks later!), he gave me the original summons as soon as he walked in the door when he got home from classes. He explained that he'd been late getting back to the car from his class, and the allowed time limit had expired at the space he'd parked. I looked at the ticket, thanked him for showing it to me, then handed it back and said, "Be sure to write a check and pay that right away." (See the rule for Chapter 5).

The parenting rule to follow is: Your teenager is an "emerging adult" who needs you to provide boundaries, limits, and a principled example. Additionally, your teenager is still your legal responsibility, so he or she remains accountable to you. Setting limits for your teenager is not only appropriate (when circumstances call for them); it is necessary for his or her well-being and development.

Three

3. Be inflexible with "rules."

When we lose the sense that we have control of things, and our anxiety rises, our tendency is to "batten down the hatches" and tighten our grip. But when it comes to teenagers, tightening the rules can quickly become a battle of wills that will keep you and your teenager stuck in "fight mode," and will prevent dialogue and learning. The third best parenting way to ruin your teenager, therefore, is to be inflexible with "rules."

We have pointed out that we need to communicate differently with teenagers than we do with children. And we've pointed out the importance of setting limits and boundaries with teenagers. But we cannot set those limits simply by setting down the law. Strictly and obediently following "rules," while appropriate for children, can become a liability when it comes to teenagers.

As we've mentioned, the best parenting postures to take when relating to our teenagers are coaching and challenging. The reason for this is that we want to guide our teenagers toward self-discipline and self-sufficiency. The parenting rule to follow is: Increase the level of freedom you allow your teenager as it is earned, but coupled with increased responsibility.

At this stage, the reason for the rules we set is more important than the rules themselves. This does not mean that rules are unimportant. They are. Parents have a responsibility to set appropriate rules for the family and its members (including themselves!). The objective is to guard against complete inflexibility on the one hand and inappropriate lenience on the other. Delivering a clear understanding of the basis for a rule helps parents avoid these two extremes.

It is normal for teens to challenge their parents regarding rules (as if you needed us to tell you this!). Putting away childish things (like childhood rules) is part of the process of becoming an independent adult. But teenagers are hindered by not being able to think maturely when trying to deal with rules they want to challenge. For example, who hasn't heard the common teen refrain, "All my friends' parents say it's o.k." The first thing to keep in mind is that the word "All" in that phrase is an exaggeration and a favorite teen manipulation tool. The second is that you know better than your teen about potential risks and outcomes in certain situations. However, it is important to avoid a terse response such as, "Well, we just don't do that in *our* family." The objective in parental coaching is for your teen to understand why things are done a certain way in your family. Merely announcing the rule is no longer enough and, as we have seen in Chapter One, amounts to *telling* rather than *asking*. As an emerging adult who craves respect, your teen needs more than that, which includes an acknowledgment that your teen now has a higher capacity to understand what is behind a rule.

Now is also the time to be clear about your standards. Your teen will not always agree (or at least won't let you know they agree) but it is imperative that you make your values and beliefs known. It may seem an exhausting exercise to always explain what, to you, seems obvious, but it is necessary for teens to consistently hear it from you. Remember, your teen is not quite an adult yet and has a brain that is still developing its capacity to recognize potential consequences. You serve an important role in pointing out how a rule matches your values and guards against unwanted outcomes. Teenagers need to consistently hear why you believe a particular rule is important or relevant to a particular situation. In this way you are really defining your guiding principles, values, beliefs and standards rather than merely laying down a rule. Your teen will come to appreciate your clarity and fairness. This will yield results later by allowing additional flexibility on your part and promoting additional responsibility on the part of your teen. Principles allow for flexibility; rules merely provide constraint. As your teenager matures, you can change the rules without giving up on principle. How much better is it for your teen to be thinking, "Am I doing the right thing?" instead of "Am I following the rule?"

An example of a rule that is ripe for endless debate is the curfew. If you feel a set curfew is reasonable then there needs to be more behind it than merely your own comfort level. For example, setting a later curfew based on birthdays is not necessarily a good pattern. It is easy to say "When you are (fill in the blank) years old then you can stay out until (fill in the blank) o'clock" but this doesn't link increased responsibility (or emotional maturity) with increased privilege. It is better to require consistent responsible behavior regarding the current curfew as a basis for changing a curfew. A teen who has consistently broken curfew at 15 and then foolishly expects a later curfew at 17 may be a teen whose parents have shown a pattern of not being clear about their values and standards. In addition, these may be parents who choose the peace and quiet of "giving in" as opposed to the rancor caused by a teen that doesn't get her way. The more parents avoid appropriate confrontation, the more firmly ingrained becomes the pattern of teens expecting, and getting, everything they want.

Another complicated situation is the inevitable rite of passage of receiving a driver's license. This event, while exhilarating for the teenager, often produces mixed emotions of pride, relief, and dread for the parent. Knowing the potential dangers of the road that our teens face is a guaranteed anxiety producer. In my state, statistics show that one in 13 drivers on the road between 10 p.m. and 1 a.m. is drunk. Between the hours of 1 a.m. and 6 a.m., one in seven drivers are drunk. Obviously driving at night puts all drivers, but especially inexperienced drivers, at risk.

When my younger son was 17 he badly wanted to go see his favorite band at a club in downtown Washington, D.C. When he came to me with this request, some important rules (and parental anxieties) were in play; prohibitions against driving in downtown Washington and being out past midnight (the concert would not end until after midnight). I could have simply taken the position that these were the rules and that was that. Instead, I chose to use the opportunity to discuss the principles behind these rules, such as earned privilege, concern for the property of others (e.g. my car) and his safety and that of others. I first explained that the rule against driving in downtown

Washington was in place because of his inexperience. Driving in Washington is a challenge for experienced drivers even in the daytime. This fact, coupled with the increased number of impaired drivers on the road at the time he would be driving, made the risk too high in my mind. He countered (with clever teenage logic) that he could not gain the required experience without being allowed to drive there. I told him that I felt his driving to date had been good and was getting better with time. However, I said, I also felt that this was not the time for him to gain unsupervised experience in such a risky situation. So, I offered a proposal that would allow him to attend the concert, satisfy my concerns, and allow some flexibility with the rules. He could take the subway into the city and attend the concert. The subway stopped near where the concert was playing. I was fortunate to have this option, but I would have been willing to drive him myself if necessary as a reward for his responsible track record. The subway, while a much safer option, still afforded a level of independence that my son desired. For some time now, my son had consistently honored the midnight curfew established for him. Since he had accumulated a large amount of trust by exhibiting responsible past behavior, I felt comfortable with him attending the concert and staying until it was over even though it would be well past midnight. I made sure I mentioned this to him as the reason for my flexibility. This satisfied him and he agreed to my proposal.

By consistently defining how my values and standards relate to the rules, my son has come to understand how his increasing privileges and independence are linked to his demonstration of responsible behavior. He does not view rules as an arbitrary parental prerogative (at least most of the time) based on my whims or anxieties, but instead sees the progression toward independence as self-earned, and mostly in his control, rather than as an entitlement. And while he is not aware of it, he's learning an important life lesson for his adulthood, because adult life works that way too.

Four

4. Expect your teenager to be perfect in everything.

The fourth best parenting way to ruin your teenager, and your relationship with him or her, is to expect your teenager to be perfect in everything. The consequence of practicing this fourth best parenting way to ruin your teenager is that you will burden your teenager with an unrealistic and unattainable expectation, and as a result, you will create an anxious and unhealthy relationship with your teen.

This is one of those patterned behaviors that originates in unexamined parental expectations. Here, the problem lies mostly and primarily with us as parents, and not with our teenager—let's be honest, as parents we want to appear perfect in our children's eyes. Several years ago I found myself working in a job and for a company that was a very bad fit. I stubbornly refused to face up to this reality and in so doing became increasingly frustrated and unhappy. My attitude caused my performance to be so poor that my boss finally came to me and suggested that a change was needed. I thought he meant moving into another position with the company. However, the change he had in mind was for me to resign and leave! It wasn't a Donald Trump "You're fired!" kind of scene, I was given a couple of months to find something else, but essentially I had been fired.

I was shocked, though I shouldn't have been. Until this point I had worked very hard to appear to others, but especially my sons, as a mistake-free successful individual. I had made my share of mistakes and had my share of failures in life, but I did not allow my teenagers to know about or see that side of my life. I said nothing to them about being asked to leave my company. Instead, I merely said I was making a change because I didn't like the job I had.

It wasn't until a good friend confronted me and pointed out that I was discounting the value of my mistakes, not only to myself but also to my sons, that I realized what I was doing. I had created a *persona,* an image, which my sons could not relate to. For them, I was someone out of reach; a person that never failed (so I made it seem) and who *expected no less from them.* My friend was able to help me see the folly of this attitude and reminded me of an important reality; we learn as much, maybe more, from our mistakes as we do from our accomplishments. I was cheating my teenagers from learning this valuable truth because of my impossible expectations. Realizing this, I came clean and told them what really happened with my job.

Their reaction was completely unexpected! They were very interested, perhaps more so than with any other event in my life. They wanted to know all the details; how did it make me feel, was I angry or sad, why did I go to work there in the first place and why did I stay there for so long when I didn't like it. They said things such as "I know how that would make me feel," "Were you scared?" "How were you able to move on?" and "Do you like your new job better?" We were connecting in a way we hadn't before. In other words, my teenagers were now relating to me as a real and imperfect human being with shortcomings just like them. The best part was telling them what I learned from the episode— that I can recover from a mistake and that it takes a courageous person to admit to a failure. Most importantly, I learned to value and appreciate the mistakes my teenagers made knowing that, handled appropriately, they provide golden opportunities for growth in their lives.

When we make our teenagers' behaviors and appearance to be a statement about ourselves (our parenting ability, our culture, our social status, our morality), that is, when we "take it personally," we distort the reality of what is going on. Teenagers are striving to find and be their own selves apart from their parents—their behavior is more about them than it is about you. Your teenagers will make mistakes on their way to becoming their own person—allow them that privilege—their mistakes are not a reflection on you.

The number one job for teens is shaping an identity—their own, not someone else's. When they emerge from their adolescence what they absolutely need to have accomplished above any other thing, is to have developed a strong sense of their own identity: who they are as an individual. This, of course, includes an appreciation for where they came from and how their family has shaped who they are. One important coaching function then, is to help your child fight the incessant unrealistic messages that our culture sends them about who they are *supposed* to be. Only to the extent that they have achieved a sense of self will they be able to tackle the next major life issue: discovering what they have been put on this planet to do, and then make vocational choices congruent with that.

Edwin Friedman, a family therapist, said that the children who navigate the maze of childhood and the turbulent waters of adolescence with the least amount of emotional and physical residue, are those whose parents made them the least dependent for their own (the parents') salvation.

It seems, then, that the more we work on being our own authentic, individual self in our relationship with our teenagers, and resist acting out of our anxiety and false expectations, and the less we try to mold our teenager into our own likeness, the better off the teenager will be.

My two sons cannot be more dissimilar from each other. A good-natured comment I often hear is "Are you sure they're brothers?" or, "Is one of them adopted?" Additionally, both have chosen career paths that are completely foreign to my own interests (or comprehension). The gratifying thing to see is how they seem to have known that they each had the permission and the blessing of their parents to chose their own paths in life. There was no expectation placed on them to follow in the path of either of their parents—and so, they were able to set their own paths while still embracing the values and principles that we tried to inculcate in them: faith, respect, responsibility, integrity, courage. Monitor your anxiety and focus on your own life goals, dreams, and aspirations. Allow your teenager to find his or her own dreams and aspirations, and then celebrate and encourage their pursuit.

The parenting rule to follow is: Allow and encourage your teenager to be an authentic human being by allowing him or her the gift and luxury of discovering his or her own self. Do not expect your teenager to be something *you* cannot be: perfect. Make sure they do not only see your "good side." Your teenager needs to see your own struggles toward maturity and growth. He or she will learn more from "overhearing" your own doubts, frustrations, deferred dreams, past failures, and how you deal and overcome these common life experiences, than from any attempt on your part to appear perfect, polished, and accomplished. I long ago discovered that my children could not care less about how many degrees I hold, how many books I've written, or how great (or "cool") other people thought I was. What they cared about most was (1) whether or not I cared about and loved them, gave them my attention, and knew about their own interests, passions, struggles, doubts, and fears, and (2) whether I would bless their own chosen paths in life.

Five

5. Take responsibility for your teenager's behavior.

One of the best parenting ways to ruin your teenager is to take responsibility for his or her behavior. And one of the best ways to accomplish this is to protect your teenager from the consequences of his or her actions. Consistently doing so will prevent your teenager from being able to learn to take personal responsibility for his or her choices. As a bonus, you will keep yourself in a state of perpetual anxiety.

The fact of the matter is that the only way to help your teenager become a responsible adult is to allow her to experience the consequences of her behavior and of the decisions that she makes for herself—both positive and negative. Those first real lessons we learn in taking personal responsibility for our decisions are formative in our lives—we tend to remember them. However much we may want to spare our teenagers from heartaches and from the consequences of poor decisions—whether because of rebellion or because of inexperience—to do so is to inhibit their emotional development toward maturity.

There are plenty of personal illustrations we can offer for this point, but if you're a parent of a teenager, you've got enough stories of your own, we're certain of that! But in case the point isn't clear enough, here are some common scenarios: if your teenager decides to be irresponsible in his or her schoolwork and is in danger of failing a course or subject, do not bail them out by making excuses or negotiating with his teacher. If your teenager loses his or her job through irresponsibility and cannot afford to pay for her cell phone or for gas for the car, don't pay her bills. If your teenager does something foolish and a police officer shows up at your door asking that dreaded question, "Are you the parent of (fill in the name of your teenager here)?" do not start thinking about how to "work the system" to bail your child out of the consequences. If your teenager fails to behave according to your expectations and according to the school behavior code and receives a suspension from school, do not make excuses for your child or demand that the school make an exception for your child. None of your excuses are acceptable: "other kids were involved too," "the school's rules were unfair," or, "my child is a good kid and didn't mean it." Those arguments do not work in real life, so don't leave your teenager with the delusions that (1) his or her behavior, intended or not intended, does not have consequences, (2) universal principles and rules do not apply to him or her, and (3) that life is always fair.

The parenting rule to follow is: Avoid rescuing your teenager from the consequences of his or her own actions—especially mistakes or acts of willful intent. I know a family whose acting-out son went to stay the night at a friend's house without the parent's permission. The dad showed up at the friend's house later to demand his son return home. When confronted by his father, the son went into a rage and kicked a small hole in the wall of his friend's bedroom. Rather than simply offering to pay for the damage and bring his son home for a stern lecture, the father called the police. The son was charged with destruction of property. At his court appearance, the son was ordered to perform community service and pay for the damage from his summer job wages. Needless to say this got the attention of the son in a way that no lecture or two-week grounding could.

Remember that the most helpful and productive parenting posture at this stage of your relationship with your teenager is coaching and challenging. The mistakes most teenagers make rarely are beyond recovery and they will survive the experience. But a string of bad experiences without the acquisition of meaningful learning leaves the teenager with less of an ability to avoid future mistakes. As I often remind my own teenagers, "Experience is the best teacher. But then you have to throw away the experience and keep the lesson learned." Rather than try to spare your teenager an uncomfortable experience, work to ensure that he or she learns an important lesson from it.

Six

6. Work hard at making your teenager your friend.

The consequence of trying to make your teenager your "friend" is that you will quickly lose your effectiveness as a coaching and challenging parent. Parents who desire their teenager to be a "friend" tend to cease being of any help to their teenager. What your teenager needs is a parent, he's got plenty of friends. Aspiring to be his or her friend robs your teenager of one of the most important resources in his or her life: the presence of a mature adult who is a role model of maturity and who can provide correctives when needed. Parents who get confused about wanting to be a friend to their teenage children are those who've fallen into the trap of emotional enmeshment. They've gotten confused about their appropriate and necessary function in the family, which includes being the *adult* in the home.

It is hard to watch our teenagers struggle through the awkward process of becoming completely independent adults, while still remaining our children. Aside from that day when we brought our first newborn home, the adolescent years may be the time when we feel most inadequate as parents.

For many of us, it is in the area of discipline that we encounter the greatest amount of stress and frustration. The problem of disciplining our teenagers is made more difficult by the fact that rebellion is a natural part of their development. In their rush to achieve independence, teenagers will challenge ideas and values held by their parents. Often, they will make shocking assertions in the process of making up their own minds about themselves, their faith, and the world in general.

I remember one young woman from a very religious home who one day declared she no longer believed in God, causing no little consternation to her parents. They wisely took their pastor's advice to not make an issue of it for the moment. As predicted, her "lapse in the faith" was short-lived. Soon the youth was back in church, participating with as much enthusiasm as ever. This scenario may have taken a different course had the parents overreacted. Of course, we can't solve all discipline problems by simply ignoring them or waiting for them to resolve themselves. The wise parent is proactive in anticipating those bumps in the road that are a matter of course in parenting teenagers. I sometimes assign parents the homework of sitting down together and making a list. On the left side of the paper they are to make a list of "the worst things my teenager may possibly do in the next three years." Then, thinking creatively, on the right side of the paper they are to write down what their most pro-active, non-anxious, responsible, and redemptive response can be to those infractions. Once they complete the list they should place it in an envelope and keep it in a desk drawer for when they need it. On the day an infraction or misadventure occurs with your teenager, it's a great resource to be able to pull out that list and hear yourself when you were non-reactive and were thinking clearly about the matter. The prescription, of course, is to follow your own advice!

Many parents ask for specific methods of punishment. "What can I do to punish my teenager?" they ask. But they are asking the wrong question. Discipline is more a matter of attitude than of action. Essentially, discipline is training for independence and maturity. Through discipline (not "punishment") you help your teenager learn to make the right choices for the right reasons. Responsible discipline is the ultimate goal when taking the challenging and coaching posture. As such, it is more valuable to understand certain principles of teenage discipline than to have a list of instant methods of punishment—notice I didn't say easier, but more valuable.

One key principle that both you and your teen need to understand is that *your teenager is still a part of the family,* though at times he or she may not believe so. While your teenager may consider herself fully independent, the fact is that until she is of legal age, out of the home, and on her own, you are still responsible for her in many ways. And, therefore, she is still accountable to you.

Understanding your teenager's desire and need to appear and feel "independent" will guide you in the tricky decisions you'll need to make in this area. While you may respect her anxiety about being seen with her parents and little sister during an outing in the mall, especially by friends and classmates, you may allow her the freedom—and option—to stay at home. On the other hand, you may rightly insist that she continue to attend church with the family. Perhaps letting her drive the car to church is an acceptable compromise that will ease her discomfort at being seen with "the family." If she seems uncomfortable being with you even at church, you may allow her to sit with her friends during the service rather than force her to sit with the rest of the family.

Never feel guilty about doing what is good for your teenager. When a rule is broken and discipline must be meted out, keep to the issue. Refuse to be sidetracked. It's nearly impossible to discipline your teenager without experiencing some resentment from him. When discipline is necessary, the issue is not avoiding hurt feelings, or keeping him as comfortable as possible. The issue isn't even his happiness. Prepare yourself to not take feelings of resentment personally, and to not feel guilty for doing what is best for him—even if he cannot appreciate it.

Most teens become adept at sidestepping the issues and causing a guilt trip for parents. Statements like, "You never let me have any fun!" or "You don't understand!" or even the heartrending cry of "You don't really care how I feel!" all have but one purpose: to make parents feel inadequate, mean, and guilty. And, admittedly, most of us are such softies when it comes to our children that we fall for these accusations—even when we know they are not true. The issue it not whether you are mean, or whether you understand. The issue is not even you; it is what your teen did to deserve the disciplinary consequence of *his* or *her* actions.

Always be consistent. The urge is to cut our teenager some slack when needing to hand out disciplinary consequences, but few teens are able to appreciate it. In their immaturity, they tend to interpret leniency as having gotten away with it. They need to learn from the consequences of their own mistakes. Sparing them from pain and disappointment may make us feel better, but it does them more harm than good.

How can your teenager learn responsibility when she's consistently being rescued from the consequences of her actions? The book of Proverbs puts it dramatically: "Discipline your child, for in that there is hope; do not be a willing party to your child's death." (Prov. 19:18). A wise parent will stick to the issue and follow through. Remember, younger siblings at home are watching how you handle your teen—they'll learn from your actions. You are setting the pattern for attitudes and behaviors that they will follow during their own adolescent years.

One of the most critical principles of positive teenage discipline is to *communicate your expectations clearly*. Make sure your teenager understands what is expected of her and what the consequences will be for infractions. When a violation occurs, you don't want to spend time interpreting the punishment or arguing the point. This puts your teen in an unhealthy position of bargaining, which can lead to an unhealthy notion that she has a say in the matter at this point. She had her say when she chose to break the rule. Contractual agreements can help, since it gives your teenager an adult sense of responsibility. The sooner you communicate your expectations, the better.

Pick a punishment or consequence that fits the violation. The discipline you choose should never embarrass or be harsh. Achieving and maintaining healthy self-esteem is one of the most important challenges your teenager will face. Attack the problem, not the person. Your teen already has to deal with peer pressure, a body that seems out of control, and feelings of inadequacy and anxiety. He doesn't need you belittling him by adding insult to injury.

Avoid becoming emotional when disciplining your teenager. Remember that your goal is to lead him or her toward maturity through your discipline. Be reasonable as you handle the situation. Nothing causes discipline to be more ineffective than to demonstrate that you cannot maturely handle your own feelings. If it helps, determine to be businesslike about it: an agreement was broken, the violator understood the consequences of breaking the agreement and chose to do so. Your teen will simply have to pay the consequences of his or her choice.

When trying to determine an appropriate disciplinary consequence, *link privileges with consequences*. Allowances can pay for the time you spent completing his unfinished jobs or chores. You may determine to make deductions from allowances for having to gather her laundry. If the garbage doesn't get taken out, deduct an agreed upon amount from his allowance. If as a consequence the garbage has to be hauled somewhere because of the missed pickup, she should pay for the gas and lose car privileges for one trip. These approaches are helpful to your teenager because they help introduce him or her to the way things work "in the real world" where adults often are fined or incur a penalty for failure to perform to expectations.

Grounding is an appropriate punishment when the matter is a question of poor time management. If low grades on a report card are a result of too much TV, announce that her time will be managed for her until some positive results are evidenced. If too much time spent hanging out with friends resulted in a missed school assignment or project, then limiting the number of evenings or weekends she is allowed to spend with friends is appropriate. For teenagers, those kinds of limits and curtailed freedoms need to remain in place for an agreed upon time, however. For example, when TV or video game limits are put in place because they affect schoolwork, then the limit should stay in place for the remainder of the school year, but not longer.

Teenagers can often appreciate when they have done something wrong. On those occasions you may want to involve them in suggesting a consequence. You may be surprised to find how hard they can be on themselves when you ask the question, "What do you think we need to do to correct this situation so that you can learn from it and remember never to do this again?"

Most importantly, *continue to communicate with your teenager after the discipline is served.* Reassure your teenager that you still love him or her. Be honest about your feelings of disappointment. Distanced from the heat of the situation, he or she will be better able to appreciate that your discipline grows out of your love and concern. And when you feel like giving in or giving up, remember to look forward to the end result of your discipline: a mature, self-assured, responsible adult.

The parenting rule to follow is: Focus on your function as a parent—coaching and challenging— toward your teenager. Work at developing your mature friendship with your spouse, not with your teenager.

Seven

7. As much as it is in your power, provide your teenager with everything he or she wants.

If you are compelled by some madness to provide your teenager with everything he or she wants, then you will deny your teenager the ability to become a competent adult who knows the value of setting and attaining personal goals and of practicing delayed gratification for higher ideals.

Trying to provide our teenagers with everything they want is a sure sign of emotional overfunctioning. Overfunctioning occurs when we attempt to take responsibility for what rightly belongs to another person: their happiness, their anxiety, their thinking, or their decisions. Regardless of our good intentions, any time we overfunction in our parental response to our teenagers—like trying to keep our teenager from experiencing disappointment, or trying to keep them "happy"—we in effect send all sorts of unfortunate messages. These messages range from, "You are incapable of making decisions for yourself," or, "You are not competent enough to provide for your own needs and wants," to "You are a dependent person who needs others to look out for you and decide what you need."

Emotional overfunctioning is a symptom of having lost sight of our core values and of our own personal goals and responsibilities. In effect, it is an invasive and willful posture that demonstrates that we are not able to distinguish between personal boundaries. In other words, we've lost the ability to know where we end and the other person begins. Parents who are "enmeshed" with their teenager perpetually invade their teen's personal space. They either try to anticipate their teenager's needs, or try to willfully inculcate their personal values, desires, and goals into their teenagers. And while it is true that we want our children to appreciate our own personal values, the fact is that teenagers need to begin to be their own person—and therefore, they must make their own decisions about the values they will live by.

When we provide our teenagers with everything they want, we in effect rob them of their ability to be independent adults who can take responsibility for their own lives. In our household, we understood this dynamic from the time our children were young. Therefore we were careful about avoiding a pattern in which they would come to believe that it was our job as parents to provide for what they wanted (providing for what they *need* is another matter. We just didn't confuse the two).

That pattern seems to have paid off now that our two boys are teenagers. Both are clear that they need to take responsibility for providing the things they want for themselves. Both have cars, but pay insurance, maintenance, and gas out of their own pockets. A few weeks ago, our youngest son reported that his car needed about $200 worth of repair for an oil leak. He mentioned this by way of information, but did not even ask for the money, saying that he was working to save up for it. Both boys have their own cell phones and their own credit cards which they monitor and pay off at the end of the month (both are determined that the credit card company will not get any of their hard-earned money merely because they cannot wait to purchase something they cannot afford at the moment.) It is clear, in watching them manage their lives, that independence brings with it a lot of self-satisfaction and empowerment.

The parenting rule to follow is: Do not confuse your own needs with those of your teenagers'. Focus on your own personal growth and maturity, on your marital relationship, and clarify the values that guide your life and relationships. You are not responsible for providing everything your child wants. In fact, you are not responsible for providing *everything* your teenager NEEDS—that is an impossible expectation. The reality is that there are some things your teenager needs that you cannot provide for him or her. There are some things that they may want—however good and appropriate—that they should work toward achieving on their own. Having to wait for something that one cannot afford at the moment is not a failure. Being able to delay gratification is a sign of maturity, not a sign of a personal shortcoming.

Eight

8. Make your teenager the primary focus in your home.

The eighth best way to ruin your relationship with your teenager, and with your spouse, is to make your teenager the primary focus in your home. The consequence of falling into this pattern is that you will maintain a perpetual triangle that will inhibit the development of healthier family relationships. It will keep your focus on your child, rather than on where you need most to focus: on your marital relationship with your spouse.

The basic configuration in relationships is the triangle. A triangle consists of three people, or two people and an issue. Dual relationships (two people relating to each other directly) are impossible to maintain for any length of time. This is because a triangulated relationship—a relationship made up of three parties—handles anxiety more efficiently. The three parties can be three persons (two parents and a teenager), two persons and an issue (two parents and the teenager's acting out, poor grades, drugs, delinquency), or one parent, a teenager, and issues around an absent parent.

The teenage years—because they are often turbulent and anxiety-ridden—seem to provide a natural and convenient source of triangles that can shape the family relationship dynamics— especially that of the parents. The paradox, however, is that when a family becomes teenager-focused, the child often takes on the parental anxiety that his or her parents do not handle well.

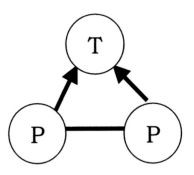

A Teenager-focused family
P=parent T=Teenager

The consequence of making your teenager (and/or his or her acting out behaviors) the focus of your marital relationship is that you will erode the primary relationship in the family: the adult relationship between the parents.

We're not suggesting that you ignore your teenager's behaviors or neglect his or her needs. As loving parents, that won't happen. You'll care for and provide well for your teenager's physical and emotional needs. But because teens take so much personal energy, time and attention, it is not difficult to one day discover that somewhere along the way your marital relationship has shifted from focusing on developing a healthy marriage to focusing on the teenager. This is detrimental to both your marriage and to your teen. The fact is that the more you invest in fostering a mature marital relationship, the more your teenager will benefit from you as parents.

Simply put, the only place your teenager will learn what it means to be a mature adult is from watching and living with mature parents. The only place your teenager will learn how to be a good marriage partner, and how to be a good parent, is from you. He or she will not learn that in school, from a college course, from their friends, or from a workshop. For example, a boy will learn about how to treat women from his father. He will learn to respect women to the extent that he observes his father treat his mother with love and respect. And paradoxically, a girl will learn what it means to be a woman from her father. Not in the sense of how to be feminine, but in the sense of her worth as a person. As the teenage girl observes how her father treats her mother—and how her mother

47

relates to her husband as partner and spouse—she learns whether a woman is an equal partner in the marriage relationship, or a convenient maidservant. And she will carry that learned concept of her own identity as a woman into her own relationships.

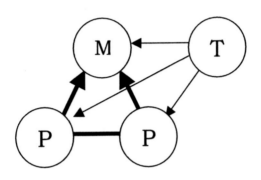

A marriage-focused family keeps the teenager out of the anxiety point

The challenge here is that parents must resist making their marriage teenager-focused. Each partner must commit to maintaining a marriage-focused relationship. Remember that dual relationships are difficult to maintain, so it's not that each partner invests in the other *person*, rather, each invests in the *marriage*. Investing in a marriage-focused marital relationship is the best gift parents can give their teenagers. This keeps the teenager out of the anxiety issues within the parents' relationship (which is something the parents need to be working on) and facilitates his or her ability to relate directly with each parent individually. And the greatest gift to your teenager is that he or she will be able to experience what a healthy, mature marriage looks and feels like.

Focusing on the marriage (rather than on the teenager) helps put things in perspective. Our job as parents is over in a brief seven years, but when we took our marriage vow it was for a lifetime's relationship ("till death do us part."). You married your spouse for a lifetime; you'll be a parent for only seven years. Maintaining a marriage-focused marital relationship will help ensure that family priorities are balanced. A teenager-centered marriage is to the detriment of each member of the family.

The parenting rule to follow is: Stay out of the relationship between your teenager and his or her other parent. Focus, instead, on the relationships to which you are directly connected—to the adult marital relationship with your spouse, and to the coaching and challenging parental relationship with your teenager.

One of the subtlest but most damaging patterns that occur with parents of teenagers is when we naively convince ourselves that our marriage (or significant relationship) is fine just the way it is. An acting out teenager in the home tends to confirm that things are not fine between mom and dad—our kids often know this before we do! Being in a good marriage is not a destination we arrive at but an ongoing process that requires constant attention. Just as a muscle devoid of exercise will atrophy, so too will a marriage that does not receive the attention and work to keep it fit, strong, and growing. There is no such thing as a marriage that cannot be improved upon, so why settle for a good marriage when you can have a great one? Focusing on making your marriage a more mature, healthy adult relationship will best serve your family, yourself, and your teenager.

Nine

9. Allow your teenager to argue with you or to show disrespect.

One of the quickest ways to ruin your teenager is to allow him or her to argue with you. The consequence of falling into a pattern in which you allow your teenager to argue with you is that you elevate your teenager to the role of a parent. Consequently, he will come to believe that he can question your decisions at any time and you will lose the respect of your teenager. Often, this pattern develops when you try to earn your teenagers' love rather than his or her respect.

When it comes to the parent-child relationship, I can think of no uglier scene than when a parent and teenager engage in a public display of a battle of wills. A parent will tell the teenager to do something and the child will argue back. Then the parent tries to reason with the teen, but the teenager still refuses to comply. Then the parent resorts to threats, but the teenager continues to argue with the parent, having learned from experience that parental threats are empty. The scary part is that the teenager's behavior indicates that he or she knows a terrible secret: the teen has learned that if she or he continues to argue and embarrass the parent, the teenager will eventually get his or her way. At the moment of engaging in that battle of wills, the parent has abdicated his or her adult parental role.

Despite appearances to the contrary, teenagers need and want to know who the parent is in the family. They intuitively know that their parents are supposed to be in charge and will find security when parents maintain their responsible family role. While they may on occasion seem to be challenging parental authority, what is usually happening is that they are testing the stability of their world—and the strength of the convictions of your values— by pushing against the edges. Their desperate need is not to win, but to confirm what they need to know: that they can count on their parents to be parents in standing firm.

Teenagers are adept at discerning what the limits are. They learn quickly that they can get away with certain things at home that they cannot get away with at school, for instance. Or, they quickly pick up that they can behave a certain way at home with mom, but they'd better not even try the same behavior at the grandparents' home, or at the home of a friend when visiting or staying over. When I was a school principal I was always amused at parents who would observe their child's interaction with his or her teacher and other adults at school and remark, "How do you get him to do that?! I can't get him to do anything at home!" Obviously, the problem wasn't so much with the child as with the adults at home. His parents had trained him one way, the adults at school trained him another, and the child was discerning enough to know the difference.

I remember, during a youth group outing of our church, giving a particular young man specific instructions for something that needed to be done. He had a reputation of being a "difficult" youth, and watching his interaction with his parents made it apparent that the source of a lot of that resided with the parents themselves. As soon as I finished giving him instructions he began telling me why he couldn't or wouldn't do it. It was an unthinking, automatic response on his part and he just kept on talking and talking. Finally, I looked him in the eye and said, "Herman, are you *arguing* with me?"

The response was dramatic. His eyes widened and his jaw hung open as it dawned on him what it was that he was doing. Then he looked at me and said, "Oh," and immediately went and did what I had asked.

As with all of these "best parenting ways to ruin" our teenager, it is when they become a long-established family pattern that they cause harm. So the key is to start training ourselves to adopt healthy parenting behaviors, and practice them consistently, while avoiding those behaviors that are ruinous to our relationship with our teen. For example, younger children should not be allowed to argue with a parent, or to question the reason why they are being told to do something. The parent may, however, choose to tell the child why they are being told to do something, and this is helpful because it teaches the child the value behind the action. A parent may say, "Mary, please pick up your toys from the living room now. We have company coming and we want the house to look nice." Or, "Billy, please give the dog a bath; he's probably feeling uncomfortable and he's unpleasant to be around right now."

When your children become teenagers it becomes more important to share the reasons why they are being told, or asked, to do something, and it becomes appropriate to negotiate on some things. If you tell your teenager to wash the car and he responds, "But I was going to go out with my friends this afternoon," it's o.k. to negotiate. You may respond by saying, "Oh, I didn't know. Thanks for telling me. But I need the car washed by Saturday afternoon." That kind of response tells your child that you respect his interests, but that you still expect him to do what he's asked.

Remember that we can no longer "parent" our teenagers. Parenting is over by the time our children are seven years old, and then we need to switch from parenting to coaching and challenging. For this reason, we need to encourage our teenager to *talk* with us on a more adult level. Teenagers go through dramatic cognitive (mental) development starting around the age of thirteen. They are able to think in ways that they have not experienced before. They discover the thrills of being able to formulate an argument and to make a case for something they want. As they make their way into a more adult world, they need practice in learning how to converse at an adult level with other adults. But they need coaching on knowing the difference between putting forth an argument, and arguing.

So it's o.k., when your teenager is seeking your permission, to allow him or her to make a case for something they want to do. A helpful coaching posture is to challenge your teenager to "convince" you as to why you should allow her to go on that trip, or to attend that event. And it's appropriate to negotiate the conditions under which you will allow it. If you and your teenager can negotiate a satisfactory common ground, then you can feel good about allowing your child to have his or her way. But if your teenager cannot provide a responsible enough rationale that you can accept, or if he or she is unwilling to accept the conditions under which you will allow a certain request, it's o.k. for you to say "No." But it's important that you help them understand the reasons why. They don't have to like it, but they deserve to know the thinking that informs your decision.

The hardest part of applying all of the "parenting ways" presented in this book will be to train yourself to respond differently than the way you may be responding currently. It helps, therefore to think ahead and anticipate what your healthy, non-reactive parental response will be when your child misbehaves or acts out.

The rule to follow is that you are the parent, and as such, you have more rights than your teenager. You also have the obligation to make certain decisions for your teenager. That's your job. Do not tolerate arguing or disrespect from your teenager—you don't deserve it and he or she does not have the right to do so. Help your teenager learn how to manage his or her emotions in a mature manner by learning how to converse on an adult level.

Ten

10. Take responsibility for your teenager's spirituality and faith.

W hen parents take responsibility for their teenager's spirituality and faith, they in effect usurp God's relationship with their teenager and inhibit the teenager's ability to develop his or her own faith.

Admittedly, the tasks of nurturing the faith of one's teenager, while not making oneself responsible for it, are difficult to reconcile. This seems to be true primarily because many of us have always been told that we are responsible for our children's faith. And, indeed, we are responsible for *nurturing* our children in faith. For many of us, that includes nurturing them into a particular faith tradition, usually in the context of a church or synagogue. But there is a non-too-subtle difference between taking appropriate parental responsibility for *nurturing* faith, and taking responsibility for that faith—the beliefs, spirituality, and relationships—of our teenager. One way can lead to a mature and strong faith; the other, however, will certainly lead to a stunted and ineffective faith or to an ultimate rejection of faith by the teenager.

Adolescence is a time when several significant developmental milestones are encountered. One very important milestone is the movement from received faith to owned faith. Teenagers still "borrow" a lot of faith, from parents, from their faith community (church or synagogue) and to some extent, from their peers in the form of values, attitudes, and beliefs. While it may be comforting to see our teenagers cling to the faith and beliefs they have acquired in their childhood, the critical need at this time of their lives is to move away from a childish, uncritical faith to an "owned" faith—one that they commit to and confess personally and of their own volition. In other words, it is no longer appropriate for them to have and hold on to *your* faith—they must discover, define, and claim their own. It is possible that in the process of shaping her own faith, your teenager may acquire beliefs that are not yours—but that is neither inappropriate nor unhealthy. Sometimes teenagers will claim beliefs that are more conservative than that of their parents, and sometimes, much more relative. The wise parent is one who is not alarmed at either, because he or she knows three things: (1) that beliefs are not equivalent to faith, (2) that as their teenager matures, so will his or her faith, and (3) that the worst thing a parent can do is hold on too tightly to their teenager by insisting that he or she "believe like I do."

Though we may on occasion wish for it to be otherwise, "teenage rebellion" is a necessary, and not unhealthy, part of the process of adolescence. Teenagers need to "rebel" against the beliefs that they have uncritically accepted from parents and their faith community to this point. That does not mean that your teenager will ultimately reject those beliefs; it just means that he or she must re-examine those beliefs and accept them on their own merit. Ultimately your teenager may embrace those beliefs willingly as something that your teen believes because he or she can affirm them, not because they are things *others* say are true, important, or worthwhile.

Just as we want to coach and challenge our teenager toward personal maturity, we need to do the same for their spirituality. A mature faith is a *critical* faith in the sense that it is not threatened by asking hard and important questions about what, and why, one believes. The fact of the matter is that the opposite of faith is not doubt, as we often assume; rather, the opposite of faith is certitude. The greatest obstacle to learning is not ignorance; it is the assumption of knowledge. Teenagers need to be encouraged to question, explore, and make their faith their own. Some teenagers can do this while staying connected and participating in the life of their church or synagogue. Others may need to do this by disengaging from participation or attendance at church for a time. This is a typical pattern for many teenagers when they leave home to go to college, for example. (Many do not return to a church until the birth of their first child, which is evidence that the importance of faith and church is not lost on them).

To say that you cannot take responsibility for your teenager's faith does not mean that you can abdicate from your parental role of spiritual leadership in the home. But like in all other areas, we must switch our stance to coaching and challenging. Experts in faith development tell us that faith (trust) is formed during the first year of life (some argue that it is formed in the first six months of life!). That is the short window of opportunity when that critical dimension of our life takes root and takes shape. To the extent that faith is formed positively, it becomes a resource for us for the rest of our lives. To the extent that it is stunted and incomplete, faith becomes a deficit in our lives— we perpetually struggle to trust God, trust others, trust the world around us, and trust in ourselves.

So, how does one coach and challenge in the area of faith? Stay emotionally connected.

Work on your own spiritual growth. Share your faith with your teenager, openly and honestly. Share not only what you are certain of and committed to and have no doubts about, but also share honestly about your uncertainties, un-resolved questions, and, yes, your doubts (remember, doubt is not antithetical to faith or to being faithful). Your teenager needs to learn from your genuine struggles with your faith. Invite, rather than insist, on church participation. Remember that your teenager has to make some important personal choices—*real* choices, perhaps for the first time. One choice many older teenagers may be faced with is whether to attend church, or to work a job on Sunday. Rather than prescribe a stance by putting your foot down on the issue, coach and challenge your teenager to arrive at his or her choice with integrity. Your coaching will be invaluable here; this will not be the first time your teenager will face a choice between his faith and his job! Help your teenager learn how to make a principled choice.

Special seasons of the Christian Year or the Jewish Year that involve occasional study and spiritual observances are a great way to invite and challenge your teenager to "pay attention" to God in his or her life. For example, your church may observe Lent, Advent, or Pentecost by offering small study groups, discipleship groups, or special studies. Inviting your teenager to join you in one of these will help you relate on a more "adult" level with your teenager. And it may facilitate some good mutual discussions on faith.

If there is one way to most effectively impact the spiritual life of your teenager, and other children in the home, it is to work on your spiritual relationship with your spouse. Remember that the primary relationship in the home is the adult marital relationship, and that includes faith and spirituality. The only place your teenager will learn how to be in a mature spiritual relationship with his or her future spouse is in *your* home, and then, only to the extent that you, as a parent, model it. Here is the scary truth: the majority of people achieve their full personal faith maturity by the time they leave home. Most adults in our culture function, emotionally and spiritually, at an adolescent level. When facing adult crisis, an adolescent faith is inadequate. The extent to which you can help your teenager grow spiritually, through your example of spiritual maturity, may be the extent to which your teenager achieves personal and spiritual growth for the remainder of life.

The parenting rule to follow is: Allow your teenager the freedom to develop his or her own faith, and take more responsibility for your own faith maturity. Trust that God already has a relationship with your teenager—let them work out their own relationship.

Appendices

Appendix A

Frequently Asked Questions

Q: "I think my teenager is using drugs, but I'm not sure. What should I do?"

A: Drugs and teenagers is a dangerous combination, and you may be fighting for your teen's life if this becomes an issue. Talk to your teen and acknowledge your suspicions. If you haven't done so already, now is a great time to be clear with your teenager about your expectations and your stance on drugs and alcohol use. Teens need to learn from you, their parents, about the risks and consequences of drug and alcohol use. Information about drugs and alcohol should not be left to a teen's peer group or the Internet. It may not seem like it, but your teen will listen to you. This is a family issue, not just an individual issue, so tell them that drug and alcohol use by teens is not allowed in your family. Tell them that they will be held accountable if they use drugs and alcohol. Then educate yourself. Find out as much as you can about teen drug and alcohol abuse.

Parents often approach talking to their teens about drug and alcohol use with dread. You may be afraid of an explosive confrontation. You may fear pushing your teen away by being too tough. However, parenting is about setting appropriate boundaries and taking responsibility, not about being liked. So have "The Talk" and be specific about your suspicions. If your teen is exhibiting new behaviors that cause you concern, or you have found drug paraphernalia in his or her room, then it's time to talk. Your teen's initial reaction will probably be to deny any wrongdoing, but keep talking; you may allow your teen an opportunity to open up. Stay calm and avoid letting the discussion lapse into an argument.

You may want to practice before your talk with your teen. You can do this with your spouse or partner. This will greatly improve your ability to have a discussion rather than an argument. Try to anticipate some of the things that your teen will bring up. For example, your teen may say "Didn't you do drugs when you were young?" If you did, you will feel awkward or guilty about this question unless you are prepared. This is not the time to lose credibility with your teen, so honesty is the best course. One possible answer is this:

> *"I took drugs at one point in my life because some of my friends did. I wanted to fit in. If I'd known then how they would affect my life, I never would have tried drugs. Knowing what I know now I'll do everything I can to help keep you away from them and help you make a decision about drugs or drinking that is good for you—not for your friends."*

Q: "My teenager was arrested while hanging out with friends. He says he is innocent and was just caught up in what the rest of the group was doing. Should I get a lawyer? Should I bail him out? Should I believe him?"

A: In nearly every circumstance like this I see the same reaction. Parents want to minimize the impact and consequences of their child's problem. Parents may at first be very angry with their teenager, but this emotion is soon overtaken by an intense desire to fix the situation. One reason parents react this way is the belief that an arrest and criminal conviction could follow and haunt their child, complicating or preventing access to certain schools, jobs or other life opportunities. In other words, their child's future will be much more difficult. It may seem counterintuitive to our impulse, but it is not the job of parents to remove difficulty from their child's experience, nor the consequences of poor choices (see chapter 5). However, it is the job of parents to help their children face up to and learn from their mistakes and failures. The arrest of a teenager will seriously challenge a parent's resolve and ability to do this but it is one the best opportunities to allow appropriate consequences to occur while working with the child toward responsibility. If parents are able to do this they will be giving their teens a valuable life gift.

I have often heard parents in this situation say to me that their teenager was "just in the wrong place at the wrong time." Other parents have said to me things such as (repeating their teenager's explanation) "He didn't know his friend had marijuana in his car." Pointing to the perceived greater guilt of others is an exercise in minimizing personal responsibility. It also is an attempt to justify parental "fix-it" behavior. Don't go there. Your teen doesn't need any excuse to de-focus from <u>his</u> or <u>her</u> actions no matter where your teenager, or you, thinks they fall on the bad behavior continuum. The issue is the behavior and choices of your teen, not that of others.

It has been my experience that juvenile courts are not out to punish teenagers beyond repair. What the juvenile courts work toward is to help steer teenagers away from risky and inappropriate behavior that could eventually escalate and lead to an irrevocable outcome. However, this is difficult if not impossible without the help of parents. If the attitude of parents is to beat the system, rather than work within the system, the long-term costs can be substantial. Such important values as "always doing the right thing" and "taking responsibility for your actions" will get lost in favor of keeping the pathway to "getting ahead" open, no matter the price.

Bail is not an issue in most juvenile arrests, but a short stay in detention often is. Any vision of juvenile detention centers as dirty, unhealthy and dangerous places is erroneous. They may not be very fun, but they are clean and safe with very strict supervision. Spending time in juvenile detention can be an enlightening experience for a teenager. Loss of freedom is the hard lesson in detention centers (which is why things such as televisions, video games, telephones and contact with friends are not available). In addition, schoolwork continues with mandatory attendance at classes held during the week. Detention gives teenagers the opportunity to contemplate the reasons for landing in this nifty resort—which, if you think about it, is what you want anyway ("Sit there and think about what you did!") but likely wouldn't be able to get your child to do at home.

Many parents hire attorneys for their teens but this is expensive and unnecessary. It also keeps the parents in "fix-it" mode rather than allowing their teens to assume full responsibility for their situation. Court-appointed attorneys do an excellent job representing juvenile defendants and your teen is entitled to one if he so chooses. This is a good decision for your teen to make independently. The court-appointed attorneys, along with the prosecutors and judges in juvenile courts, have seen it all and are very good at arriving at appropriate consequences within the limits of legal guidelines. Second chances are almost always given in the form of reduced charges, community service and stricter curfews, with a chance to clear the record if all these requirements are properly satisfied. Juvenile court judges are adept at constructing these second chance penalties with stern caveats that the original, more severe punishments, await those who make the mistake of repeating behavior that brought them into the court system in the first place.

It is very important for parents not to treat a first-time offense by their teen as an anomaly. The phrase "Surely this won't happen again" is often a false hope. The best way to ensure a repeat offense doesn't happen is to treat the first transgression as seriously as you would a second or third and let your teenager feel the full weight and consequences of their choices from the start. Remember, it is rarely the one-time event that shapes a destiny, rather, it is the patterned ways of relating and behaving that does.

Q: "My teenager is spending nights away from home without our permission. She refuses to tell us where she is staying. When we press her on the matter, she threatens to run away. How can I deal with this without risking that she'll follow through on her threat?"

A: This is an extremely complicated and difficult situation to deal with. Before addressing this very serious situation, let's step back a bit and first talk more generally about curfews.

Set curfews that you feel comfortable with, not what your teens demand. I know of very few teens that express satisfaction with their curfew; so don't get sucked into their persistent pleas or the "everyone else is allowed to" whines. A curfew is a chance to give teens greater independence within a structure of clear expectations. So be explicit about the connection between this greater independence (later curfews) and expectations (consistently honoring the agreed curfew, being honest, showing respect, being responsible with their time). Blanket curfews are appropriate but allow some leeway for when they have something special or you need them to be home earlier.

Always ask for and receive information on where your teenager will be and with whom. Call the parents of friends you don't know. "I'm going out, see ya!" is not enough information from your teen. She should be very clear about her plans and should call later if she wishes to change them and move locations. This works both ways, so you should also be in the habit of letting your teens know where you will be when you go out. Tell your teens it's not just about trust but also about accountability and respect for each other. Don't allow your teen to call 15 minutes before curfew to ask to sleep over at a friend's house. This kind of hurried request should be a "something's up" red flag. If your teen doesn't comply with all your requirements tell her that she is not allowed out due to her lack of responsibility. And follow through!

However, occasionally a teen will act in troubling ways such as staying out all night without permission. There can be many reasons for this, such as being with others, or escaping to places that are distractions from the problems in their lives. It can also be a warning sign for other risky behaviors like alcohol and drug use or sexual activity. A teen that threatens to run can paralyze a parent into inaction. However, action in this situation is required. It is too dangerous to do nothing.

Set aside time to have a conversation with your teen. Prepare what you wish to say and stay calm. Avoid raising your voice or yelling even if your teen is raising her voice or yelling. Ask your teen why she is staying out. Agree that if she will respond to you, you will stay quiet until she is completely finished explaining. Then be quiet and listen. Understanding your teen is the objective here, not agreeing with your teen. When your teen is completely finished responding to your question, tell her you love her but that you cannot allow her irresponsible behavior to go on. Continuing to stay calm, and without raising your voice, let her know she has exceeded the boundaries of what is acceptable in your family. Tell her you understand her feelings but that she must deal with them in a more appropriate way

In the event your child does start staying out nights, contact every possible location your teen may be staying. If you think she is staying with friends, call their parents and tell them your teen is there without your permission. If things continue, it is critical to seek professional help. If family counseling fails, then seek the help of the local police and/or the court system. The rules vary from locality to locality but usually the police and courts are more than willing to work with parents in this situation. Try to establish a relationship with a patrol officer in your area. In my jurisdiction, any minor that fails to come home on two separate occasions can be picked up and either brought home or taken to an intake officer at juvenile court. This often gets the attention of teens. Intake officers can be very helpful in explaining what the court system can do to help parents with an uncontrollable teen.

Some parents can feel completely at a loss in such circumstances. It can be a very lonely experience, especially if you believe you are the only one dealing with such issues. It can also be difficult to admit to such a problem because of embarrassment and a strong sense of failure. However, it is a very courageous parent that can ask for help. You would be surprised at how many parents struggle with similar problems and do not get help because of embarrassment. But embarrassment is too high a price to pay for the safety of your child, or for your own peace of mind. Seek out and join a parent group to learn from, and share information with, others in similar situations. A parent group can help eliminate the false notion that you are the only one going through this and can provide you with invaluable information from those who have been there before you.

Q: "We suspect that our teenager is sexually active, but we don't know for sure, and don't know who he or she may be having sex with. How can I approach my teenager with this?"

A: Let's start by making this simple confession: it is not possible for parents to make sexual decisions for their teens or to control their teen's sexual activity and relationships. So, finding out that your teen is sexually active does not mean you have somehow failed. However, you can still be a very important and positive influence on your son or daughter's sexual decisions. You are the best source of information regarding the truth about sex and your goal of being a good parent should include being the *first* source of this information. Discussion of sex among a teen's peer group is often ridiculously distorted making it imperative that you open a discussion about sex early so your teen can get the facts. Waiting until you already suspect your teen is sexually active will make beginning such a conversation extremely difficult.

The statistics regarding unwanted pregnancies are alarming, further emphasizing the urgency of this topic for family discussion with your teenagers, and yes, your children. The best prevention against unwanted pregnancies is knowledge and correct use of contraceptive methods such as condoms. It is of course appropriate for parents to discuss abstinence and many teens do choose abstinence. However, the reality is that most young people become sexually active by their late teens. Some of the reasons for this have been around for generations, including:

- Peer pressure
- Natural, and healthy, biological urges
- Confusing sex with love
- Curiosity
- Rebellion
- Pressure from a boy/girlfriend
- A need to feel loved.

In addition, our current popular culture opens up a whole world of hard-to-ignore sexually suggestive material through television, movies, print media and the Internet. So, it is imperative that parents stay actively engaged in addressing this topic with their teens. This is no time for a "head in the sand and hope for the best" attitude. You can allow the culture to "educate" your teenager on sexual values, or you can choose to take that responsibility. Doing nothing means you've abdicated that responsibility to Hollywood, television, popular culture, or your teen's peer group—all of which are very eager to educate your teenager on sexuality.

Don't wait for your teen to start the conversation. Make time now to discuss and give some simple advise regarding sexual activity. Begin by letting your teen know you are available at any time to have a private, frank, one-to-one conversation. If you are uncomfortable talking about sex, admit it. Knowing your willingness to have the discussion despite your discomfort will reinforce its importance for your teen. Share your values regarding sex. If you feel a person should wait until marriage, say so, but also be ready to deal with the possibility that your teen may choose to have sex before marriage anyway. Tell your teen to ALWAYS practice safe sex. Obviously, a pregnancy is many times more likely if a sexually active teen does not use a condom. This tends to be a difficult stance to take for some religious parents. But remember, you cannot control your teen's sexual behavior, nor can you *will* your teen to adopt your values or conform to your desires concerning his or her behavior. The danger here is falling into the trap of getting "SITS" ("Stuck In The "Shoulds"). Deal with the reality of the situation you're facing, not with how you think your teenager "should" behave. Let's admit it, you don't live how you "should" either—you know you should pray more, be kinder, save more money for your retirement, eat healthier, lose some weight, give more to charity, do more for the less fortunate, and attend church more regularly. You "should" do all these things, but you don't. So don't get stuck in the "shoulds" when dealing with your teenager.

Since it is potentially life threatening to your teen you should resolve to talk about sexually transmitted diseases (STDs) including HIV/AIDS. If you are unclear about STDs, educate yourself in advance so you can pass this knowledge on to your teen. Some experts suggest that if you believe your teen is unlikely to wait until marriage, you should encourage monogamy. Having only one sexual partner greatly lowers the chance of being infected with an STD.

Listen to your teen's thoughts and feelings and answer their questions respectfully. If you perceive your teen to be too uncomfortable to ask a question face to face, suggest that he or she write you a note. The more comfortable you can make the experience, the more likely your teen will continue to approach you about the topic of sex. I know of one parent who carried out this conversation concerning sex through e-mail and instant messages. It was a good start that led to an ability to talk openly person-to-person with his teen.

Like every aspect of human relationships, our faith, our religion, and our values help guide us toward healthier ways of being and living. Be clear about what you believe about God's gift of sexuality and the values that your faith tradition encourages in this area of life. By maintaining a clear and respectful dialogue regarding sexual activity, you will be in a much better position to ask your teen if they have become sexually active, and to know how to respond redemptively. Let your teenager know that your questions and concern regarding their sexuality comes from a place of genuine love and concern and not just because you are nosey. Tell them that, although you may not approve of them having sex, you want to remind them of the potential pitfalls that you have discussed with them. Remember, although you cannot control your teen's sexual activity, you can be a healthy and mature influence in your teenager's life if you work at it.

Appendix B

Discipline Guidelines for Teenagers

1. Set realistic and reasonable limits for your teenager.

2. Be consistent in your discipline

3. Accept your teenager's feelings, which he or she cannot control, but do not allow disruptive and destructive behavior.

4. Correct your teenager's behavior with love and respect.

5. Never knowingly or intentionally embarrass your teenager.

6. Do not force your teenager to say "I'm sorry."

7. Avoid threats (they are meaningless if you cannot follow through).

8. Notice and acknowledge your teenager's good behavior.

9. Do not force your teenager to give up something he or she enjoys as a means of punishment.

10. Help your teenager feel that she can talk to you openly and without risking a "lecture."

11. Give emotional support to your teenager by being "present" and showing an interest in the things he or she enjoys.

12. Allow your teenager to gain wisdom from experience by not rescuing your teen from the consequences of his or her actions.

13. Give encouragement freely.

14. Do not feel guilty about making a tough decision or providing a strict consequence when warranted by an infraction.

15. Allow your teenager to have his or her own opinion, but demand and expect courtesy and respect.

16. Keep issues with your marriage separate from your relationship and the discipline issues with your teenager.

Appendix C

Parenting Advice From Teenagers

We asked a group of teenagers for their advice to parents on how to raise teenagers. Here's what they said (unedited!):

"Don't be so overprotective. The whole world isn't out to get us . . . let us live a little."

"When I'm crying or mad, clearly I don't wanna be bothered. So <u>don't</u> try to talk to me."

"Don't hinder the life lessons I will learn from my mistakes."

"You've taught me well, go on that. Trust me and my things. I know when "too far" is."

"I'm not you, I can't be. I won't necessarily make your mistakes, so don't try to make me or say that I will."

"I don't tell you things because you won't understand, but that doesn't mean I have something to hide."

"Don't tell other parents about my business, that's why it's MINE!"

"Be patient when I drive."

"When we're not in a good mood, leave us alone!"

"Let us fight out our problems with our siblings, it makes us feel better."

"Let your kids wear the clothes they want to."

"I would say, just love them and have some control but let them make their own mistakes."

"We're going through almost the same thing our parents did. So, they need to understand when we make a mistake."

"There are other ways to get us to understand we were wrong than yelling and screaming or grounding us for months."

"Give your kids more freedom. Let them live their own lives and make their own mistakes."

"Don't get mad over one bad grade."

"Spend as much time with them before they grow up."

"Female teenagers always feel very insecure, mostly about the way they look. So I would suggest maybe try to boost our confidence by complementing."

"Try to let us have freedom. I know we don't always make the best decisions, but let us learn from them. Believe it or not we do learn from our mistakes and will not repeat them."

"If we're feeling down usually we want some time to ourselves."

"It's good to keep watch on us, but don't suffocate us. Just as you did, we (as teenagers) need to experience the things you experienced, to learn from the mistakes we make."

"Give us freedom when it comes to what we are able to do, but make us face the consequences of our actions."

"We still love you no matter what we say or how upset we get. We still need you at times but we also need to figure out who <u>we</u> are, and how to deal with life."

"We still need you, but we also need to learn how to live <u>without</u> you."

"Don't be so concerned about everything I do."

"Parents should get the message when they are embarrassing their offspring."

"Don't get too involved in my problems. Just listen and if it gets out of control and I ask for help, then help me out and get involved."

"Don't be so protective."

Bibliography

Caldwell, Elizabeth. *Making A Home for Faith: Nurturing The Spiritual Life of Your Children.* The Pilgrim Press, 2000.

Canter, Lee. *Assertive Discipline for Parents.* Harper & Row, Publishers, 1985.

Galindo, Israel. *The Craft of Christian Teaching.* Judson Press, 1998.

Galindo, Israel. *The Bible, Live! Experience-centered Learning Activities for Children.* Judson Press, 1999.

Galindo. Israel. *Let Us Pray: Contemporary Prayers for the Seasons of the Church.* Judson Press, 1999.

Galindo, Israel. *The Tree of All Hearts: Modern Parables for Teaching Faith.* Smyth & Helwys, 2000.

Gauld, Malcolm & Laura Gauld. *The Biggest Job We'll Ever Have: The Hyde School Program for Character-Based Education and Parenting.* Scribner, 2003.

Gilbert, Roberta. *Extraordinary Relations.* John Wiley & Sons, 1992.

Gilbert, Roberta. *Connecting With Our Children.* John Wiley & Sons, 1999.

Ginott, Haim. *Between Parent & Teenager.* Avon Publishers, 1969.

Gottman, John. *The Heart of Parenting: Raising an Emotionally Intelligent Child.* Simon & Schuster, 1997.

Rekers, George (ed.), *Family Building: Six Qualities of a Strong Family.* Regal Books, 1985.

Richardson, Ron. *Family Ties That Bind.* Self Counsel Press, 1999.

Silverman, Marvin and Lustig, David. *Parent Survival Training: A Complete Guide to Modern Parenting.* Wilshire Book Co., 1978.

Strommen, Merton P. *The Five Cries of Parents.* HarperCollins, 1993.

Strommen, Merton P. *The Five Cries of Youth.* HarperCollins, 1985.

Strommen, Merton P., et al., *Passing on the Faith.* St. Mary's Press, 2000.

About the Authors

Israel Galindo is the author of several books, including *10 Best Parenting Ways to Ruin Your Child,* and is Executive Director of Educational Consultants. An educator and author, he is a former school principal and former hospice chaplain. Currently he is a professor at the Baptist Theological Seminary at Richmond. He is married to Barbara and they have two boys, one grown and gainfully employed, and one who is in college.

Don Reagan lives in Fairfax County, Virginia, with his wife Ruth. They are the parents of two sons, ages 21 and 18. For the past several years he has been a leader in a parent support group connected with the Hyde School, a character based secondary boarding school. In addition, he is a participant in the Fairfax County Juvenile Court parent group through which he assists and mentors parents of teenagers.

OTHER BOOKS BY *Israel Galindo:*

10 Best Parenting Ways to Ruin Your Child
With wit and humor Dr. Galindo presents the most important parenting missteps to avoid.

The Craft of Christian Teaching.
This essential book on Christian teaching focuses on ways to becoming a VERY good teacher. (Judson Press)

Myths: Fact and Fiction About Teaching and Learning
A fun way to challenge our mistaken notions about teaching and learning. (Educational Consultants)

The Tree of All Hearts.
A collection of teaching stories and parables. (Smyth & Helwys)

Let Us Pray.
Contemporary and poetic prayers for all occasions. (Judson Press)

The Bible Live!
Experiential learning experiences for children and youth. (Judson Press)

The Hidden Lives of Congregations.
Understanding church dynamics and leadership. One of the "10 Best Books of 2005", Academy of Parish Clergy. (Alban Institute)

A Christian Educator's Book of Lists.
A handy compendium of information, facts, helps, and knowledge for teachers and educators. (Smyth & Helwys)

Teaching Handouts *(e-book)*
A collection of over 200 handy teaching handouts in the area of education, instruction, parenting, church history, theology, and Bible study. (Educational Consultants).

Most of these books are available on Amazon.com or through your local bookstore. Or, you may use the order form on the following page.

ORDER FORM

To order additional copies of *10 Best Parenting Ways to Ruin Your Teenager,* complete and mail the form below or submit your order by e-mail to: **igalindo@aol.com** (ask about multiple copies discounts!).

SHIP TO:
Name: _____

Address: _____

City, State, Zip code: _____

Day phone (___) _____

____ copies of	*10 Best Parenting Ways to Ruin Your Teenager*	@ $12.00 each:	$_____
____ copies of	*10 Best Parenting Ways to Ruin Your Child*	@ $9.95 each:	$_____
____ copies of	*The Craft of Christian Teaching*	@ $16.00 each:	$_____
____ copies of	*The Tree of All Hearts*	@ $15.00 each:	$_____
____ copies of	*Prayers for the Church*	@ $5.00 each:	$_____
____ copies of	*Let us Pray*	@ $13.00 each:	$_____
____ copies of	*Myths: Fact & Fiction about Teaching & Learning*	@ $13.00 each:	$ ____
____ copies of	*The Bible, Live!*	@ $12.00 each:	$_____

Postage and handling @ $1.55per book: $_____

Virginia residents add 5% sales tax: $_____

TOTAL amount enclosed: $_____

Make checks payable to:
Israel Galindo
11904 Rutgers Drive
Richmond, VA 23233